Reginald Rowland

An Ambitious Slave

Reginald Rowland

An Ambitious Slave

ISBN/EAN: 9783744732819

Printed in Europe, USA, Canada, Australia, Japan

Cover: Foto ©ninafisch / pixelio.de

More available books at **www.hansebooks.com**

AN
AMBITIOUS
SLAVE

by
REGINALD ROWLAND

The Peter Paul Book Company
Publishers . Buffalo, N. Y. . 1897

AN AMBITIOUS SLAVE.

CHAPTER I.

"OH! Massa John I neber took it. Lawd, Massa John I neber."

"Well you'll take this I reckon, and it'll be many a long day before you have another chance to take anything else from the wagons, or my name aint John Mason, for I expect to make you drive the foremost team hereafter, where I can ride along and keep my eye on you. It hasn't been three weeks since the Judge bought you, and in that time there has been one box of shoes, two cheeses and a whole coop of chickens stolen from the wagons. Now take that" giving Rufus a farewell cut with the whip as though afraid he would not give the

supposed thief his full share of punishment for the loss of goods from the
wagon train, adding in a voice of vehe-
mence, which made the flesh quiver upon
the bones of the darkey, "I might have
known a nigger fresh from the plantation
would have jumped at every chance to
steal anything he could get his hands
on."

The foregoing represents a portion of
a dialogue which took place between
John Mason, the foreman of a wagon
train, a hard master and a slave perse-
cutor, and Rufus, a colored man scarcely
more than twenty years of age, who had
recently been purchased from a planter
and brought to the town to drive one of
a long train of wagons carrying freight,
baggage and all kinds of produce between the terminus of the only railroad
entering Augusta, Ga., and the station
in Hamburg, just on the opposide side
of the Savannah River.

This was in October, 1844, when very

few were the mills of progress which had rumbled out upon the still air of the "Sunny South," and a score of years before the wave of Freedom had swept over the States setting a million souls at liberty. The exercise of will, to a large extent, and reliance upon their own judgment was totally unknown to the "niggers."

All freight, baggage and express was transported between Augusta and Hamburg by means of a wagon train driven by colored men, then slaves, and an overseer on horse-back at the head of the train, with one also bringing up the rear, passing over the Savannah River on a wooden bridge, and which in those days was the only available means of communication directly between the two towns mentioned.

It was not an infrequent occurrence for a driver near the center of the line of wagons, watching his chance, and while neither overseer was in sight, to drop from the dray for instance a box of shoes, (provided he was sure that he could depend upon the driver immediately behind not betraying him) which was received by an accustomed hand at pilfering, who was ready to conceal the goods taken.

It was frequently the case however, that a more trustworthy slave, or possibly one who had been hovering a grudge against the thief, would report the matter, and the stolen article would be recovered, even if the rogue had not been detected by the watchful eye of the overseer.

Rufus was as black as a crow, and had a broad, flat nose, which is an unmistakable mark of the native African, although he was somewhat taller than the average man. He had been bought from a planter who owned a large cotton plantation, and who declared to the purchaser that "the like of Rufus couldn't be found in airy cotton field in the State," while his new boss recognized in him an aptitude for loading and unloading his freight wagons, the contents of which were often piled to a considerable height.

One evening after the slaves had brought in their teams, eaten their plain but much relished supper, and had gone to their humble shanties to dream possibly of a land where there were no bosses and the sound of the whip was never heard, a short and always grinning darkey called Sambo, who had a saucy twinkle in his eye, came to John Mason, to whom it had just been reported that a coop of chickens had that afternoon disappeared, and opening his broad lips as though he could accommodate a few of the feathered tribe there, says, "Boss, I know where dem chickens went," and upon being asked regarding their mysterious departure, continued with a grin of satisfaction "Rufus dropped em off at 'Tilda's house. I seed him, Boss."

Rufus was at once brought upon the scene, whipped until his hard master felt satisfied there would be less goods stolen in future, and rewarding Sambo for his faithfulness, Mason instructed him to keep his eyes open while working near Rufus, who in reality was not the thief.

Several days passed, during which time Rufus attended strictly to loading and unloading his dray, while Sambo, according to instructions, drove the team immediately behind him.

The mischievous and domineering Sambo would occasionally attempt to joke with Rufus, but the latter, like an Indian whose dignity had been severely wounded, failed to manifest great pleasure in the presence of his fellow slaves, and once when Rufus had piled box upon box in his wagon, he completed the load by placing a coop of chickens on top. The long wagon train had just left the bridge, while constant jolting over the rough roads had caused the

coop to work its way to the back of the
wagon, and Rufus, fearing it might fall,
ran back as the team moved slowly
along and began placing the coop in its
former position. Sambo, who was watching the procedure, quickly ran up and
offered his assistance with the taunting
remark, " here, country nigger, better
let me help yer handle dese yer chickens. First thing yer know they'll be
gone." Rufus accepted his assistance
but made no answer, which displeased
Sambo, who continued "Whaffer yer so
quiet since you and Boss Mason come
'quainted ? "

The following morning at an early
hour, John Mason was standing in the
office of Judge Walton, the owner of the
wagon train, receiving instructions regarding a large shipment of drygoods
consigned to a Hamburg merchant, to
be handled, when a slave came in and
in a very excited manner, informed them
that Rufus was missing and that no one

on the premises had seen him that morning.

For the next hour excitement ran high throughout the "negro quarters," while Sambo stood by listening with a serious expression upon his dusky countenance as though he was ashamed of the record he had made in not being first to bring the news of Rufus' departure.

The *Daily Recorder* on the next morning, and for a week thereafter, contained the following notice:

RUNAWAY NEGRO. From the premises of Philip Walton, one buck negro six feet high, twenty years old, very black, close cut wool and scar across left hand. Reward offered for his apprehension.

Day after day passed and no tidings of the runaway slave reached the owner, and John Mason was instructed to take the morning train down to Maxton and visit "Squire Longside's" plantation, being told not to return until he had captured Rufus or was satisfied that he had not returned to the farm, to which

Mason replied, suggestively tapping the handle of his rawhide whip upon his right hip pocket : " If I ever lay my eye on that nigger I'll bring him back, though he may not be able to work when he gets here."

The last few words were said in an undertone, and did not reach the ear of Judge Walton, which was well for Mason, as he knew, for while the Judge was very positive in dealing with his subordinates, he was a very humane man, and many were the hardships the slaves suffered at the hands of their " Boss " which were unknown to their owner.

The laws of the State prohibited any one teaching a negro even as much as the alphabet, and while some people recognized the sense of feeling in the negro, the vast majority ignored that sense, and not a few of the more hot-headed type declared " the negro has no soul, and will not exist in the hereafter. I can detect the odor of one a half mile distant, and nothing that is so offensive can last."

According to the Judge's instructions, when the morning train left Augusta south-bound, Mason was aboard accompanied by Arnold, Judge Walton's son, who was home from school on vacation, and to him this was considered the greatest outing trip he had ever known —after a runaway negro.

CHAPTER II.

IT was nine o'clock in the evening, when in a typical log cabin, about one hundred yards from the main road, leading up to 'Squire Longside's plantation, sat Dinah and Ned beside a bright light made by a pine knot in the broad fire-place—the chandelier for the cabin—while two little pickaninnies had cuddled upon a low bed in one corner across which the flickering lights and shadows played hide and seek. They were perhaps dreaming of the water-melon time which had recently passed.

The cabin door was open and as the breeze of an October night occasionally fanned the flickering blaze, Ned and Dinah were discussing their daily topic —Ole Massa's cotton crop.

The "Squire" provided comfortably for his slaves, although their quarters were ever so humble, and here was a picture of happiness difficult to equal among more pretentious surroundings, as the darkies occasionally sang in their peculiar tones a verse such as :

" I wake up at de break of day to take my morning walk,
I meet my lobely Judy and dis de way we talk—
Says I, you am my only lobe, you am my heart's delight,
Wont you come across de riber, and we'll habe a little dance tonight."

and Ned kept up a thump, thump, with his banjo, which is ever music in the negro's ear;

"Listen," said Dinah, "Sho as de Lawd somebody's dyin' cause I heard a voice way off say 'D-i-n-a-h.' Shut dat door, Ned."

Dinah's superstitious theory was suddenly exploded however, when a head appeared in the doorway, and Rufus asked to be given food.

"Whaf fer you come back here," exclaimed the head of the family, "doan

yer know yer treadin' on dangerous
groun'." While Dinah went straight to
the cupboard and produced what remained of a pumpkin which had been
roasted in the ashes, inside of which had
been cooked a 'possum, but very little
of the latter remained to satisfy the
fugitive's hunger.

When Ned and Dinah retired, which
was long after the rooster had told of the
midnight hour, Rufus had received their
promise to not disclose the fact of his
presence on the old plantation, and he
was wending his way down a narrow
path through the field, where he could
see enough of the fleecy staple ungath-
ered to cause a sigh of regret to pass
from his humble lips, as he was reminded
of all the familiar scenes—the day he
was sold and parted with all that had
become dear to his youthful heart, for
although it was night, he recognized
every turn in the old path, and every
knoll which rose in the distance like
mountains against the clear sky.

Rufus followed the path for nearly a half mile, and turning to the right he continued through a little ravine for about a hundred yards, when he came upon a steep bluff thickly covered with shrubbery. Making his way through the bushes he soon came to a deep cavity in the side of the hill in which he had the night previous prepared a bed made of brush and dead leaves, covered over with cotton. Directly in front of this cave was a great swamp, and being so obscure Rufus felt safe in making his abode in the cliff.

CHAPTER III.

JOHN MASON and Arnold left the train at Maxton Station, and hiring a mule and buggy, which was public conveyance for the town, reached the plantation of 'Squire Longside, where they found all in gay attire as the 'Squire's daughter was to be married at nine o'clock the same evening ; every one was busy making preparations, and full of jovial excitement.

Constance Longside, the bride-to-be, was much admired among the country swain, not a few of whom had sought her hand, and among the unsuccessful suitors was one Clarence Dawson, who was the owner of a small farm adjoining that of the 'Squire.

To say that Clarence was wild with rage when he learned of the coming marriage of Constance to a planter who lived miles away, is mildly expressing his feelings, for while he had known Constance all his life, his rival had only met her a few months previous, and he considered she was being taken right from under his nose, as it were.

The wedding had been the talk of all the country folk in the neighborhood, and even the slaves were wondering what Clarence would do when Constance, the source of his hopes and ambitions had gone, and he could no longer hear her evening song mingled with the tinkling sound of cow bells, while he rides up the adjoining lane bring the lowing herd to shelter for the night.

Dinah was the only darkey heard to express sympathy for Clarence, but Ned, with a degree of pride which was characteristic of a slave owned by a well-to-

do man, asked: "Wha' you think
Missie would wanter marry po' white
trash like Clance fer?" The condition
coveted next to being free, was to be
owned by a person in good circumstances, consequently it was a joke
which Ned never tired of telling, and
which he availed himself of the first
opportunity to tell to strangers, that on
one occasion, when he had been owned
by the 'Squire only a short time, the
latter passed him one morning in the
road and failing to recognize Ned, asked
who was his master.

The hour for the wedding found the
country home well crowded with friends
and relatives of the contracting parties.
In the parlor, or the "big room" as the
negroes termed it, plain chairs which
were in keeping with other quaint furniture of the house, were arranged on all
sides, with the exception of the door and
a broad "fire-board," with its very odd
decoration composed of cedars bearing

balls of cotton varying from the size of a
pigeon's egg to an orange, some dyed
with "poke" berries and others yellow
with the yolk of eggs. Large bunches
of golden-rod adorned each corner of
the room, while in the center was sus-
pended a cluster of mistletoe heavy
laden with its pearly berries, which latter
adornment was the object of much com-
ment among the superstitious country
young folk ; it was an old superstition
which had been handed down from one
generation to another, that the couple
who sat beneath the fatal mistletoe were
destined to form a matrimonial contract.

Just opposite the mantle, a door which
was all but blocked up with homespun
frocks of waiting maids, led into a narrow hall and thence into the kitchen
where could be seen the supper table
well laden with the best edibles the
farm produced, including the wedding
cake, a portion of which each of the
curious spectators anticipated dreaming
over that night.

John Mason, who learned that Rufus and Ned had been the best of friends, decided to remain over until the following day and keep a watch out during the festivities ; therefore he and Arnold were ushered in, also the disconsolate Clarence, who was extremely reticent, as every one seemed to notice to his discomfiture, awaited the appearance of his rival to claim and bear off his lost love.

Clarence on this occasion, with a final effort to appear to advantage before the girl he had almost worshipped, had entered his garden and pulling the only rose left, whose companions had from time to time made their way to the bosom of Constance, placed it in his buttonhole, and strode off in a pair of new boots with toes turned up and long-tailed coat, buttoned high under his ears, to join the gayer crowd. In reality there were no few "sheep eyes" cast at him by maids whose bloom of youth was considerably on the wane, and who might be said to be blooming alone, but he felt if the sweetest smiles of them all combined were bestowed upon him, they would not suffice for the one he had lost.

The wedding, which was performed with little ceremony, was soon over, and after the company had departed, with the exception of a few intimate friends who remained over to accompany the bride and groom the next morning, Mason quietly sought the house of Ned, and to his joy there found Rufus seated at a table with his colored host and hostess enjoying a portion of the wedding supper.

Mason reached for his revolver, and with eyes gleaming like balls of fire in the darkness, started to enter, when a hand was placed upon his shoulder and he was told to put up his pistol and do nothing rashly. It was Arnold who spoke, whose words were heeded by Mason at times when no one else could influence him, and feeling less desperate,

Mason turned, and picking up a willow branch, which was lying just across a ray of light from the cabin, he entered, led his captive out who made little or no resistance, and before the laughter of the wedding party had scarcely died out, he chastised the runaway slave until he begged on his knees for mercy.

Mason led Rufus back to what the negroes called the "big house," the scene of the gayeties, followed by Arnold and Ned. He demanded the latter to bring him a rope, which was quickly produced, and tying the captive to a tree, heartlessly remarked, " now stay there until morning, and the man who tries to release you sooner, will have me to settle with."

"What!" asked Arnold, "have you no more feeling for humanity than to keep him there bound to a tree all night? Besides, some one will release him before morning."

"Yes," was Mason's retort, "I have

some feeling for *humanity*, but that nigger dont leave that tree until to-morrow, when I am ready to leave."

" John Mason," replied Arnold, " if you leave Rufus bound there all night, it will be the most expensive act you ever indulged in, for you will certainly have a successor in the service of my father when he is made aware of your conduct."

Mason dropped his head with a sub-dued look and realizing his position, requested the 'Squire, who had been attracted to the scene, to give him a room which could be securely locked, in which to place Rufus for the night.

The slave was carried to a small " shed-room " in which was an old mat-tress, the use of which had long been abandoned, pieces of broken furniture piled in one corner, and a shelf bearing several old pictures which formerly adorned the walls of the house ; and there he was locked up.

Every one on the premises retired, including Rufus, but he could not sleep, and as he lay in the darkness, his mind reverted to old-time scenes on the plantation, which he would again be compelled to leave. He could see in his imagination the field white with cotton until it appeared as a vast snow scene, and a dozen or more darkies singing some favorite melody while they filled the baskets with the fleecy staple. Thus Rufus lay half awake, half dreaming, until he was startled by a harsh voice at the door telling him to rise.

CHAPTER IV.

" They hunt no more for the 'possum and the coon,
  On the meadow, the hill and the shore.
They sing no more by the glimmer of the moon,
  On the bench by the old cabin door."

IT was morning, and after all had breakfasted, Mason, Arnold and the runaway slave drove off to Maxton, the nearest railroad station, seated in one of the 'Squire's conveyances, just as the bride and groom, accompanied by several friends, drove in the opposite direction toward the bride's future home.

Two persons were leaving beloved surroundings—one the bride, as happy as the lark whose musical call pealed out upon the morning air, while the other, a slave, who had been maltreated on the premises of his new owner, had fled for liberty, been captured and was returning to be cuffed at the pleasure of his hard master, or strictly speaking, his Boss, in the person of John Mason.

The three boarded the train, and Mason placing Rufus next the window, sat on the inside to prevent his escaping through the door, while Arnold took a seat further forward.

They were riding in a primitive old car which rattled and jolted along with very little more speed than the team in which they had driven from 'Squire Longside's farm. The conductor, who was as lean as the mythical razor-backed hog, collected their fares, acted as brakeman, got off at every small town to turn the switch, and at one station coupled on another car to be carried up to Augusta.

In the meantime an old, country lady, accompanied by her granddaughter, a rosy-cheeked girl probably fifteen years of age, came in, and the small car being crowded, Arnold offered a portion of his seat, which was taken by the lass, after the old lady was seated just opposite. The maiden was somewhat bashful, and Arnold attempting to make her feel at ease, tried to draw her into conversation. But the girl appeared absolutely unaware of his presence, until he looked her in the face and asked if she was going far. The blushing maid, to the astonishment of Arnold, sprang up as though indignant, and crossed over to the old lady, who came back to occupy a part of Arnold's seat where her granddaughter had been, as Arnold thought, to give him a "piece of her mind," but in reality only to inform the frightened lad the girl was deaf and dumb.

The old lady wore a bonnet in which were placed a couple shanghai feathers (which evidently had been plucked from a tale of woe, as will be seen) which she had probably worn since a girl, judging from their appearance, and were of such a length as to keep Arnold constantly dodging, in order to prevent their coming in contact with his eye.

The car suddenly turned a curve in the road and the old lady throwing her head to one side as Arnold leaned forward, the longest feather in her hat struck him straight in the eye. It was undoudtedly painful, and shutting his eye tightly, he threw his head back, when the feather and hat parted forever, for Arnold cautiously threw it (the feather) out the car window.

The grandmother became somewhat ironical, for as she left the car, she was heard to remark to Arnold if he ever should wear glasses it would not be on account of weak eyes, still bemoaning the loss of her feather.

The three reached Augusta by noon, and soon poor Rufus was the object of a jeering crowd, piercing him on every side with humiliating remarks, the most sagatious of whom was the irrepressible Sambo, who saluted him with a grin: " Spose you's decided chicken 's better'n 'possum since Boss Mason was onto yer."

Mason had recited to Judge Walton his experience in capturing the slave, and just outside the office was met by his fellow overseer with whom he managed the wagon train, who, after listening intently until Mason had finished, rejoined as though he disliked to be outdone " we've also had a little excitement here since you left. That big fat nigger Jake gave me some of his impudence yesterday, and in return I gave him the but-end of my jack-whip. It's all over though, we buried him out at Oakwood, but his smartness cost me a team and the work of two niggers for three hours."

The excitement quieted down, and as the weeks doubled into months and months into years, the wagon train made its daily run to Hamburg and return with such regularity that not the slightest complaint reached the ears of the gray-haired Judge, through the iron-hearted Mason, although the latter per-

son could not lie down at night and en-
joy what he called the sleep of a man
who had passed a dutiful day, without
his daily routine of abuse, which con-
sisted of a threat of punishment on the
least provocation, accompanied by a cut
with his rawhide whip (let it fall upon
whom it may,) in order that the slaves
might more appreciate the fact that their
hides remained unbroken, and they were
living in our "land of the free."

Mason was a man who saw little
morality in the world, nor had he any con-
ception of a higher realm of existence,
but his ambition and fields for new
acquisitions lay in the heathenish con-
ception of overpowering whatsoever was
physically inadequate to withstand his
onslaught.

An idea of the nature of the man may
be drawn from the following incident:

Christmas was drawing near, the
freight had assumed unusual propor-
tions, and in order to accomplish the

greatest possible amount of work in a given time, he offered a prize to the slave who would load and unload his wagon in the least time and keep it up for one day, in consequence of which every negro did his utmost. At the close of the day's work he called them all together, and after delivering the prize, warned each man that if they did not make an equal record every day, he would treat them to the cowhide.

One night a half dozen or more slaves were at the house of Dinah, to whom Rufus had been accused of delivering the stolen goods, some lounging about the dingy room in various postures of rest, while others more enthusiastic over the subject being discussed were standing. Several of them were giving their respective opinions as to the time which might possibly bring freedom to the slaves.

They had heard of a man named Lincoln who had been stirring the Capitol with his speeches on anti-slavery, and Rufus, who was lying in a corner of the room unnoticed by some, listened intently to all that was said, while in his unconquerable yearning for freedom, that night he recognized a star of hope in the northern horizon, which he resolved in his untutored mind to follow.

The morning of December 23d was bright and almost as mild in that sunny climate as the month of May. Several darkies obtained leave for a couple of days to visit relatives and spend the holidays, one of whom was Rufus, who carried a carefully folded paper in his trousers pocket signed by Judge Walton, in possession of which he felt that no one would dare question his right to be traveling alone.

In no section of our country was Christmas ever celebrated with so much merriment and fun-making as in the South in those days, particularly among the slaves, according to the extent to which the master's approval was given. Christmas in the South was more like the Fourth of July further North, for while the latter was also a great day for "young America" in the South, its festivities were not equal to those during the Christmas holidays.

CHAPTER V.

"I'm a happy little darkey all the way from Alabam',
I used to hoe the cotton and the cane,
The white folks they will miss me when they call for little
    Sam,
For I'm never going to live with them again."

THE day after Christmas, when business houses had resumed their duties, a crowd was seen gathering around a small brick building in Alexandria, Va., over the door of which were painted the words "Price, Berch & Co., Slave Dealers." A number of slaves were to be disposed of at public auction, and it was understood there were several bargains awaiting some one with the ready cash.

On the right of the house was built an annex with iron bars across the windows—a typical slave-pen in which the "stock" of the company was kept—

which bore close resemblance to a country jail.

Among the slaves who were held as chattels, was an old colored " Auntie " and two little darkies six or eight years of age, who were continually asking her " Mammy, where is we gwine' ? "

" Doan yer bother yer mammy, chile, I's gwine away today, and maybe de white folks make me leave you chilluns here," then adding by way of consolation to her little ones, who were not aware that they would probably be sold away from their mother, " Mammy'll come back though and see her chilluns 'fore long."

The first upon the block to be bid upon was a boy about eight years old, and while the auctioneer was trying to convince his hearers there was never such a favorable time to buy, a strange looking negro might have been seen to turn suddenly as he came into full view of the crowd and quietly disappear around the corner, but the eyes of all were upon the auctioner, and Rufus was not detected.

He had reached Alexandria the previous night, and stopping where it only remained to cross the Potomac to be out of Virginia, he had not anticipated a scene such as met his eyes.

Night settled down upon the quaint old town, and as the fast express just from the South passed out of the marshes and on to the long bridge spanning the Potomac leading into Washington, a passenger sat, weary of a long ride, looking out into the moonlight eager to catch a glimpse of the great light upon the dome of the Capitol, signifying that Congress was in session. He saw only for an instant a face which impressed him with its familiarity, though he tried in vain to place it.

It was Rufus sitting upon the bank of the river, looking out on the silvery waters as the thousands of waves danced in the moonlight, and thinking of to-morrow when he hoped to unfold his tale of sorrow before Lincoln, and from whom he fancied he would receive some hopes of freedom, but the slave was not aware that the train which passed him bore into Washington an intimate friend of Judge Walton, who being a Representative from Georgia, would likely recognize him if they should come face to face in the Capitol, although the slight gleam of light from the car had not been sufficient to betray the fugitive.

For many days and nights Rufus' humble mind had pictured the City of Washington as a City of Refuge, and as one pauses upon the eve of a great struggle and endeavors to recognize at least a shadow of the events the next few hours may bring, he paused upon the threshold of the city.

Hundreds of small lights on the distant streets were twinkling across the water, while the great light upon the dome of the Capitol supported by the

Goddess of Liberty, seemed to be beckoning and bidding him enter the city and be free.

The following morning found Rufus on the streets of Washington, and he tried to assume the air of a negro who was familiar with every block in the city, but if passers-by failed to notice the expression of undoubted pleasure which the sights of a city always bring upon the face of a country darkey, he could not evade detection when his clothing gave indications of a tramp who had fared anything but well.

Looking from under his slouch hat, Rufus suddenly saw he was within a few yards of the Georgia Representative whose face was familiar to him upon the streets of Augusta, and frightened almost out of breath, the slave darted into an alley and cautiously made his way down to the railroad yard where he remained throughout the day in an empty freight car, not daring to again venture out in the city in daylight.

CHAPTER VI.

"All up and down de whole creation,
Sadly I roam,
Still longing for de old plantation,
And for de old folks at home."

THE heart of the slave sank in despondency when he thought of his danger of being caught if he remained in Washington. Having abandoned the object of his trip, he looked out from his place of concealment upon the stars twinkling just as they did upon the old farm, and he began to wonder if there was no place where mercy could be found for a slave—one who in fleeing for freedom had transgressed the law by which he should go through life manacled. Was there no place where the white man would employ him as a hired servant? Was there no black man whose freedom had been purchased, and who thereby valued it sufficiently to be willing to give shelter to a refugee? Oh! that he could behold the face of the man who had individually undertaken the task of arguing the case of liberty for the manacled thousands! Thus bemoaning his fate, the disappointed Rufus fell asleep in the empty box car from sheer exhaustion.

The following day Rufus reached Boston, having been carried out of Washington while asleep, and he soon found many sympathizers among those to whom he related his escape.

The refugee felt that the vast number of miles that lay between he and his "Boss" afforded him absolute safety, hence he did not hesitate to tell of his recent experience in the Capitol and his hunger since he left Georgia, all of which appealed to the charitably inclined, which formed a large portion of the curious listeners.

Time and again had the Boston
papers heralded stories of runaway
slaves, some of whom were "carried
back South only to have the lash applied
to them with an attempt to eradicate
their longing for freedom," which might
or might not have been true, but here
was one right in their midst.

Rufus was persevering in his one
ambition—to be free—and while he had
gained nothing by his visit to Washington, he thought of a story which had
been told him of the building of a
tower :

When a little boy heard that a great
tower was going to be erected a block
or two away, he insisted on being carried
to see the work in progress, where his
juvenile mind had pictured a tower of
the "Jack the Giant Killer" type, run
up in a couple of days. But was disappointed to find an excavation in the
earth which he termed "a big well."
Whereupon it was explained to him the

greater the building in height, the deeper the foundation is laid, in which Rufus found consolation from the fact that what sometimes appears to be trouble may end in rejoicing.

One morning Judge Walton took up a newspaper and glancing over it, his eye fell upon the story of Rufus, which had been copied from a Boston paper, the result of which was that he immediately left for Boston, and finding his long sought slave, prepared to carry him back to Georgia, which brought down the condemnation of the City of Boston upon the Judge.

On the night following the arrival of Walton in Boston, the citizens held an indignation meeting and denounced the slave-holder in strong terms, declaring that he should not be permitted to carry Rufus back. Prominent citizens expressed their respective opinions before a demonstrative crowd in the old Town Hall, with the result that a committee of three was appointed to call upon Judge Walton and inform him that he would not be allowed to take the refugee back into slavery. The old Hall roared with applause when such a resolution was announced, and the Committee immediately proceeded to find the Judge, while the meeting awaited their return, but upon being called upon by the committee, the Judge avowed his intention of leaving Boston with his captive on the following morning.

The enraged Judge having locked Rufus up securely, returned to the Hall with the committee, where he argued that the slave rightfully belonged to him by law, and the same law that empowered him to enter another state and bring back a runaway mule, if it was proven to be his property, also gave him the privilege of apprehending a runaway slave and carry him back to serve his master in slavery, no matter where located.

The law favored the slave-holder, and after a hot discussion, the committee proposed to pay a reasonable price for Rufus' freedom, before he should be made a slave again, reciting Rufus' version of the treatment he had been subjected to.

"What valuation do you place upon the slave?" asked a member of the committee, addressing the Judge.

"Five hundred dollars," was his reply, whereupon the committee as in one voice, joined by a chorus of the spectators, declared his price was exorbitant.

The Judge drew from his pocket a list showing quotations in the slave-market, and particularly the price he had recently paid for a "Buck" negro, presumably of corresponding size and age to Rufus. He was offered four hundred dollars for the man by way of a compromise, which was finally accepted, and the amount was made up at once among those who vehemently avowed their disapproval of the Judge's action, and the crowd dispersed.

Rufus was indescribably elated over his freedom, and soon found employment on an old vessel which was originally designed for slave traffic, but was remodeled and was then being used in the lumber business, plying between ports on the eastern coast.

The captain was a grim old veteran sailor, who delighted in reciting to his only colored subordinate, stories of the days when he brought hundreds of the young "blacks" to America, and of his narrow escape from the natives while relieving them of the care of their offspring, which he related in a coarse voice, broken by an occasional chuckle. Describing the wailing of the "pickaninnies" as they were borne away from the savage country, he appeared to find great pleasure in reminding Rufus of the bondage of his race, probably to make the ex-slave more appreciate his freedom.

CHAPTER VII.

RETURNING to the scenes which our freedman had deserted ; in what seemed a few short years, we find Arnold Walton converted from a smooth-faced youth at school, into a full-fledged politician, stumping the District on the questions of the day. He admonished his hearers in the name of patriotism to exercise the right of American citizenship, vote his ticket, and thereby save the country from drifting into the hands of a ring of unprincipled law-makers.

Arnold rapidly grew into public favor, and the result was that on election day he was overwhelmingly declared the people's choice to represent the District in the National Congress, where he proved to be ever on the alert to strike a blow against the Anti-Slavery question which was being agitated by the representatives from certain States, and which Arnold termed a move to rob the South of a legitimate industry for purely political reasons, turning thousands of ignorant mortals who possessed no idea of management (the most intelligent of whom had not a vestige of executive ability), out upon the world to earn a livelihood.

Upon a visit to Boston during his Congressional days, Walton was invited to deliver an after-dinner address before the Commercial Club, some members of which were desirous of hearing a man from the South whom no few looked upon as advocating inhuman persecution, and whom a comic paper had described as "having wheels in his head, which he utilized to crush out liberty and life."

A sight in those days unusual in the

North, attracted Arnold's attention while seated at the dinner-table on that occasion, as he glanced down the long double line of members and guests arranged on either side of the sumptuously spread table, engaged in satisfying the inner man. It was a single black face among the waiters, whom he recognized as Rufus.

The stroke of the town clock told it was drawing toward the wee sma' hours, and a line of carriages the entire length of the block were waiting to receive the dispersing banqueters, when Arnold felt a hand placed upon his arm as he left the club-house. Looking around, he beheld Rufus.

"'Skuse me, boss, but I jus' want to speak to you 'fore you go, and ask about old Massa Longside, and all dem."

Arnold was touched by the sincerity of the ex-slave, who still remembered one who treated him kindly, and when

the negro was told that 'Squire Longside had a year ago joined the silent
majority, his eyes filled with tears.
Rufus possessed an unusual aptitude
for service in any capacity as a slave,
while the story of his freedom rendered
his name familiar to every person in the
city, hence when he heard that Walton
was to attend the banquet, he experi-
enced no difficulty in being engaged for
the occasion, his only object in which
was the scene just described.

CHAPTER VIII.

"WHEN THE CRUEL WAR IS OVER."

NEWS of the closing bloody strife between the states, by which slavery was abolished, reached the ears of Rufus like a heavenly anthem, and though in a few years he would have passed over the sunny side of life, he now looked out upon the future where the sunshine of hope was just penetrating the clouds, and gleaming over a land strewn with desolation. While added years had rendered him less impulsive in his sole ambition, and though his kinky wool was becoming prematurely gray, the knowledge that even his former companions were as free as himself, was a joy, too great for him to remain hidden in the obscure ranks of humanity without at least making an effort to see the promoter of this boon to his race, to whose service he would gladly have devoted the remainder of his years. Such was the gratitude that lay hidden in the breast of Rufus. He accordingly bid farewell to the Captain of the lumber craft at Norfolk, with whom he had just made a trip from Boston, and purchased a railroad ticket destined to Washington, feeling that he could now visit that city with an unlimited degree of impunity, where he expected to pay homage to the liberator of the slaves—the President.

At No. 601 "G" street, Washington, stood a one-story frame building, being a lunch house kept by an old colored woman who accommodated probabaly a half dozen transients of her race when she was fortunate enough to have her house filled, in which Rufus engaged a room for a couple of days. This house, or mere shanty, for such it was—was constructed in the most inexpensive manner possible, the rear of which was simply built against the side of a somewhat larger building, while the entrance to the latter was on Sixth street, being just around the corner from where Rufus was stopping. Thus the side of the larger building, which was also a frame house, formed the rear of the smaller one, just where Rufus' room was situated.

Rufus immediately proceeded to retire upon his arrival, which was close to midnight, but though he was fatigued from his traveling, he could not sleep on account of an annoying voice which seemed to come from a distance.

The night was still and quietude settled down upon the city, while the sound of footsteps on the street had dwindled down to an occasional belated pedestrian. The occupant of the dark and scantily furnished room lay awake trying to overcome his fear and superstition connected with the voice which he could not account for.

It came like a stage whisper from the most repulsive villain, which he at one moment imagined came from the ceiling, and the next instant was positive the same sound emanated from beneath his bed. Rufus could control himself no longer, and raising to a sitting posture, he listened to the voice which had become less distinct, when he observed a tiny ray of light penetrating the rear wall. He very stealthily approached the rough partition and found the light came from the adjoining building through a hole in the decaying wall, which was so small as to have possibly been made by a clothes hook, and listening to the voice which had so annoyed him, Rufus heard the name of the President mentioned.

Whether it was for his undying and insatiable interest in the name that reached his ear, or because of mere curiosity born in the human race, Rufus spent an hour endeavoring to catch the conversation going on in the adjoining room.

The words were very low and cautiously spoken, but once he caught this much : " Mac thinks he intends going to the play tomorrow night, and will try to find out in the morning when the family are at breakfast. If all goes smooth until tomorrow night, we will bring him down."

Here the conversation ceased, and while Rufus did not realize what was meant, the words "we will bring him down" kept ringing in his ears. He reasoned in his humble mind, "It can't be Massa Lincoln who dat man talk 'bout bringing down to dis har house."

When Rufus again opened his eyes to the light of day, the sun had mounted high in the sky, for he had slept late. It was a calm morning on the 14th of April, just such a day as makes us yearn to leave the house, within whose walls our sphere has been to an extent limited during the winter hours, but which on such a morning becomes al-

most painfully monotonous, and our
attention is drawn to the outside world
where we can breathe the air of freedom, bask in the sunlight of returning
Spring, and learn a lesson of renewed
hope as we listen to "Nature's Teach-
ings."

The philanthropic African felt the in-
spiring influence of such a day, and
while preparing to make his exit from
the scene of an unrestful night, a voice
was heard which he at once recognized
as the same which had disturbed his
sleep the previous night, the first sound
of which was a premonition of evil, and
he shuddered as he recalled the demon-
like whispering which came through the
wall, and which still haunted him.

With an eagerness to learn more of
Mr. Lincoln and why his name should
have been connected with a secret conversation in such an obscure lodging,
Rufus noiselessly resumed his position
by the defective partition, where he

could now hear nearly the entire conversation of the two men, who seemed to entertain little or no fear of being overheard. Rufus heard the voice of a man who seemed to be out of breath as he entered the room and took a seat near the wall. The man who was within a couple of feet of Rufus, proceeded to inform his co-operator exultingly of what he had accomplished.

"That block-headed coachman," exclaimed the man who had just entered, "kept me waiting in the stable nearly an hour, and gave as his excuse that the servant-girl failed to turn up in time, but if he has not told me a lie, which I will admit I don't remember his ever doing, everything will go off like clock-work tonight. He says the old man will be in a box tonight, and have the ladies with him."

Rufus, who was listening intently, did not know who was referred to as "the old man," but "whoever it was," Rufus said mentally, "I would not like to depend upon that man helping him out of a 'box' if he should get in one," as that slang expression recurred to him.

"Well, what about the horse," reached the ear of Rufus, which he recognized as a woman's voice.

"Oh! the horse will be there, and that at ten o'clock sharp, or that coachman will suffer for it," was the answer.

"I shouldn't wonder if he makes a nice botch of the whole affair, and if he does——." Here the woman paused, as if considering her own risk in the plot she was having executed.

"Why, then every man will have to look out for his own neck," resumed the male voice, "and as for you—the jailer will probably look after that for you. However, after everything is arranged, I must have the money planked down, before I put my hand in the fire."

"And even after I turn the money

over to you, how do I know that *you*
will not also slip up in the game, and
skipping the city, leave me to settle
with the detectives, and no money,"
argued the female.

"The matter is arranged; when all
eyes are upon the play, I will enter the
box, make short work of it, and out the
back alley where the horse will be waiting, and before any one outside knows
what has happened, I will be half way to
Sur—"

The speaker was suddenly rebuked
by the woman, who advised him to
lower his voice, or he would be over-
heard, with a sad result.

CHAPTER IX.

"THIS man wants to speak to the President," said the watchman at the White House, addressing the President's Private Secretary. "I have been unable to get any more information out of him than that fact."

"*This* man!" exclaimed the Secretary, looking at Rufus somewhat surprised. "Why old man unless your business is of an extremely important nature, you cannot see him. What do you wish done?"

The ex-slave appeared slightly confused, for it had never occurred to him that there would be any question or difficulty in his seeing Mr. Lincoln. "Please Boss," he commenced, "I jes'

want ter thank him for settin' all dese
niggers free."

The Secretary's expression assumed
a more surprised look, and a smile
showing that he was somewhat amused,
crept over his face, as he informed Rufus
that the President was occupied, and he
would have to be satisfied with leaving
his card, (with a wink at the watchman),
while Rufus turned and went slowly
away.

The disappointed darkey was on his
way to his lodging house, when he was
passed by two school boys on a corner,
one of whom inquired of his companion
if he was going to attend the theater
that night, and upon receiving a nega-
tive reply, informed his friend that he
was going, as he wanted to see the
President, who was going to occupy a
box at the play.

Here an idea occurred to Rufus which
almost straightened his curly wool, as
he at once connected with the President

all he had overheard through the wall in his room, and he was satisfied there was a plot being formed to harm the Chief Magistrate.

Let come what might, Rufus resolved to save the President from his conspirators, and turning he started back toward the White House as fast as it was possible for him to move.

Night had just come over the quiet city and the cool breeze from the Potomac river sighed among the branches of the large maples surrounding the "White Lot" as the President's carriage drove through the broad gate and down Pennsylvania Avenue.

It had not proceeded far when "Police!" a man cried, "Police, Police!" and from every direction people were seen running to the center of the street to where the carriage had halted. "Arrest that man," cried the driver, as several policemen ran up, and seizing a man who had attempted to stop the carriage, dragged him away to the jail.

Rufus had made a daring attempt to warn the doomed man, and as he was carried off after failing to do so, the carriage proceeded, while the negro repeatedly cried "stop the carriage, stop it, they may kill him," but the policeman who had arrested many supposed cranks, said the man was demented, and carried him to the station house, where Rufus spent the night locked up.

Ford's theater, which was in the early days of Washington, *the* theater of the city, was situated on 10th street, N. W. between "E" and "F" streets, which building is remaining today.

The theater was profusely decorated with stars and stripes in honor of Mr. Lincoln, and as he entered the house, which was well filled, round after round of applause rose from the mass of humanity, and the President, unconscious of his impending fate, was ushered into the box on the left of the stage.

If poor Rufus could have appeared upon the scene at this moment, he might at least have given warning of what was to follow in the next few minutes, but alas ! his being unexpectedly dragged from the carriage and unceremoniously cast into jail, so completely unnerved the African, that before he could recover presence of mind sufficient to recount the plot he had over-heard, the murderer approached his victim from the rear, pressed the fatal trigger, and almost before the audience realized what had happened, sprang from the box to the stage, disappeared behind the scenery, and making his exit into the back alley, mounted the horse which was in waiting, and disappeared in the darkness with the swiftness of an arrow.

CHAPTER X.

WE will turn back to scenes among the hills and valleys of Georgia. In the spring of 1865, if we could as an eagle in the air, view the country, we would find the roads over hills and through valleys dotted with disbanded Confederate soldiers returning home.

Two of these men had walked the entire distance from the field of Appomattox, with scarcely more than the uppers of their shoes left upon their feet. One of them wore only the crown of a hat, while the other wore a cap which had been picked up on the battle-field, reaching Chickamauga one morning just as a special train was about to leave for Atlanta, which was to transport what remained of a regiment of soldiers.

The two tired "Rebs," who still carried their muskets, were boarding the train, when they were confronted by the conductor, by whom they were informed very gruffly that he could not accommodate them.

"But we can stand just here on the platform," replied one of the two tired men, "where we will take up no room which is needed, and we are only going to Cartersville."

"You must get off; I will have no room for you," shouted the conductor, who knew neither of them had as much as a penny in his possession.

"Oh! we will not be in the way here," argued the spokesman for the two.

"Get off! get off!" shouted the conductor, at the top of his voice, while the two "Johnnies" only clung to the car and calmly replied, "No; we couldn't think of doing it."

"Come in and sit down, then!" said the conductor, as his anger seemed to turn to mirth, "make yourself comfortable, if possible."

The perseverance of the two men who had nothing more to lose but a life upon which neither placed but little value, was comical in the extreme, although their situation was deplorable.

The conductor was a man from the Union army who had been placed in charge of the train. When his train slowly moved off toward its destination, the conductor took a seat near the "Confeds" and jocularly remarked, "Well, my friends, you seem to be in rather a bad plight, but it is better to see your error late than never at all. You were evidently on the wrong side of the fence."

"If the side of the victorious is always the side of right," rejoined John, your assertion is true, but I claim the reverse in this case.

"But, my friend," resumed the conductor, "does loyalty count for nothing?

Do any circumstances justify a man in fighting against his country?"

"I claim they cannot," answered John, and I never could be disloyal to the extent of fighting against my natal land."

"Were you not raised a citizen of the United States, and when you entered the army," continued the conductor, "was it not to fight against the Union?"

"I fought in the Confederate army, but I believe a State had a right to secede after years of Congressional wrangling had proven that the differences of opinion were such that we could no longer form a part of the Union ; as my State is the nearest and dearest to me, I could not take up arms againt it, and there is where I lay claim to loyalty."

As the old Southern soldier was thus trying to disabuse the conductor's mind of the assertion that he had been "on the wrong side of the fence," the train drew into Cartersville, where the two

Confederates got off and resumed their homeward tramp through the mountains. Clarence Dawson (for it was he who had been arguing with the conductor) on a hot July day the previous summer had been wounded on the battle-field. A comrade gave him the last drop of water from his canteen and otherwise contributed to his comforts until the wounded man could be carried from the field. Clarence never forgot this little act of kindness, and when the war had ended and he, heartbroken and disconsolate, started on a long journey home, which he only trusted had been spared from the ravages of the invading army, he by chance came upon the crippled soldier who rendered him such timely assistance. It was now Clarence's time to show his true comradeship, and when his cripple companion left the train at Cartersville to seek his cabin in the distant mountains, Clarence insisted that he would never leave the old soldier until he saw the hands of the rural mountaineer clasped in fond embrace of those loved ones who were still watching and wondering the fate of the son and brother who had upon that sad morning bid them farewell with tears in his eyes.

The sun went down, rose and set again, and Clarence with his cripple companion wended his way through the rocky, mountainous country. Clarence still carried his gun (which to the day of his death he treasured as a memento of those days of struggle) and often while climbing a rugged hill would put out his hand and assist his almost helpless comrade, who had long since been compelled to discard gun, blanket and all except what scanty clothing were upon his body.

As they neared the home of the wounded man, he seemed to imbibe new strength and pushed forward in renewed hope, as his watchful eye was scanning the hills before him for a trace of smoke which might tell of life on the old premises.

At last only a little knoll in the battle-scarred wood lay between the two men and the spot where the crippled man was longing to rest his eye and eventually rest his body, but instead of Clarence now rendering assistance, he found it difficult to keep apace with his comrade. They mounted the hill among the debris which gave evidence of a fierce battle, and rushing impatiently down in full view of the once familiar spot where he expected to find home, only a vast plain of desolation met the eye of the wounded man, and he sank upon the ground. Turning a face of anguish toward Clarence, and while unable to utter a word, he expired upon a scene where devastation held full sway.

The cabin had months previously gone up in smoke, a storm of shot had almost swept every trace of habitation before it, and a death-like silence reigned supreme in the scene of awe-inspiring solitude.

Clarence alone followed a mountain road for a half hour, finally coming upon a small house, he procured a man and necessary implements with which they dug a final resting-place for the remains of the heart-broken veteran.

As they laid him to rest, the dead man's coat fell open and disclosed a portion of a Confederate flag under which the soldier had fought, and which he had cut from the staff on which only remained a remnant of silk bearing two stars, after the gradually fading Star of the Confederacy had gone down forever upon the field of Appomattox. Clarence divided the piece of cloth, placed a piece bearing one star upon the body of his departed companion as he was hid from mortal eye, carefully folded the other half and placing it in his coat pocket, started back toward the nearest railroad station, but not without shedding a tear for the man with whom he had shared the hardships of war.

CHAPTER XI.

"All the world's a stage,
And all the men and women merely players,
They have their exits and their entrances,
And one man in his time plays many parts."

THE tumult into which the Capitol City was turned at an hour of merriment, and the excitment which prevailed throughout the night, with the dawn of day, relaxed into a calm and reverential silence. People not only were loth to discuss the tragedy, but many walked the streets with a soft tread, apparently afraid to breathe aloud.

From the night of April 14th, 1865, for many days following, if we could view the city as from the crest of a distant mountain, we would observe a cloud of mourning rising from the center of Washington and spreading with increased gloom on every side, until a vast canopy of crape hung over the Union. Even the great American eagle seemed to rise with wings outspread, and through respect to the Nation's dead exclude the light of gaiety from the outside world.

A report of Rufus' experience in trying to stop the carriage, and his immediate arrest, reached the ears of the detectives, who sought the cell of the ex-slave and probed him for information until he had related all he heard transpire between the conspirators, and upon being released from confinment, he conducted them to the room he had lately occupied. The officers went from there to the adjoining building, one room of which was only separated from Rufus' apartment by a defective wall, and there arrested an old woman whose voice Rufus declared was that heard from his room. The officers there found a clue which resulted in the capture of the assassin.

*　　*　　*　　*　　*　　*

We will turn from a page of horrors, to happier days in the life of Rufus.

> " The mightier man the mightier is the thing
> Which makes him honored or begets him hate,
> For greatest scandal waits on greatest state."
> —*Shakespeare.*

Jonesboro formed a suburb of Augusta, the residents of which were colored, with few exceptions. Down on a sandy flat where the waters of the Savannah had apparently swept over the land in days gone by, stood rows of small cottages and cabins, above which rose the spire of "Zion" Church, and with a couple of stores and old shops, the whole formed a negro village.

On one occasion when the residents had stopped work on Saturday noon (for neither money or pleading could prevail upon a negro to work on Saturday afternoon) those who had not gone to the City for supplies which could not be procured from their small stores, were lounging around the corners, enjoying their freedom. A dark stranger made his advent, who soon created a commotion among the dusky residents. A few of the older among them recognized Rufus, whose escape had been recited to the younger generation until he figured as a hero in the minds of those who had never seen him.

On the following day when the little human cloud rolled out of "Zion," an enthusiastic circle was formed on the street corner, with Rufus as the center of attraction, while the crowd was swelled by all the corner loafers, curious to see the new-comer.

"What all dem folks doin'" asked one whose attention had been attracted by the boisterous talking, "must be somebody got happy down there."

"Dat dar's ole Rufus," replied the darkey to whom the inquiry had been addressed, who was on his way home to spread the news. "De man what all dese folks been talking 'bout, who run'd away when he was young, de Yankees bought him free, and after all dis time he come back when we're all free."

Rufus came like a Rip Van Winkle into Jonesboro, except that there were more living who remembered him than were left to recognize the mythical man of the Catskills, although time had frosted the wool on the ex-slave's head. Rufus became the leader of the negroes who for miles around flocked into Jonesboro to hear the fascinating tales of his experience. Thus the new-comer soon became eligible to any gift within the power of the negro faction.

After a couple of years had passed, during which time Rufus was endeavoring to fit himself for more usefulness, the hero of Jonesboro was chosen by the darkies to represent in the City Council a Precinct in which they were able to control the ballot.

How this indominable being ever

obtained the rudiments of an education, was a mystery to all who knew him, but by his insatiable search for knowledge, Rufus became able to electrify those who heard him speak in public, which was a marvel to the whites, and a source of ecstatic pleasure to the negroes.

He delighted in advising his followers regarding their future, and once argued : "fellow creatures, we have been slaves together, we have been bound in subjection as with one great shackle, but the hand of an omnipotent Being has cut asunder the bands of servitude, and pointing to a distant land, bids us cross the water and on yonder island of the sea, establish a monarchy which coming years may hold up to the world as a model form of government. The negro has filled his mission (though an involuntary one) in the United States, for, coming out of slavery we see his color is against him, and our only sucessful future lies in colonization.

"A white man might emerge from slavery, go out into the world and mingling with his own race, his identity as a former slave is lost sight of, but not so with the African—he may move from city to city, migrate from State to State, but people will look upon his black skin and say 'there is an ex-slave' and thus while his years of bondage are recalled from the dead past, he is recognized as the equal of no man except the day laborer."

Thus we find Rufus pointing out what he thought to be a more glorious future for his race, but his plan was too slow materializing for his ambition upon earth to be realized.

"My brothers," he continued, "a messenger of freedom has been sent us, which rose like a star in the sky, and shedding its light upon every slave in our broad land, shone there in splendor until we were all guided out of bondage, then like a pilgrim whose mission has been filled, receded into the heavens, leaving the responsibility of our future upon our shoulders.

Should we, like birds which have just passed through the door of the cage into our natural element, remain near the scenes of our long confinement? No, we should shake the dust of the cage from our wings, and rising in unity, seek a new and sunny clime."

When Rufus could gather even a dozen listeners behind closed doors where he could agitate the cause for which he pictured a glowing future, he would reach the height of enthusiasm over his project, but his followers dropped away until they became so few that he was almost alone in his cause. Indeed his popularity was on the wane, which he realized, while the entire cloud which was darkening his political horizon had emanated from the question of his marriage contract.

When his term expired in public office, Rufus had gained the favor of the colored faction, and his name as the leader of his party so generally known, that when he suddenly, and for the first time in his eventful life decided to venture into matrimony, he found no difficulty in gaining the hand of a white woman, who was willing to share with him the snug fortune he had acquired.

The choice of his wife was a death stroke to the political career of the African, for while the white censured his wife for uniting herself with a negro, his own followers deserted him for not honoring his own color by choosing from their ranks a partner for life.

At this period a great change came over the life of Rufus. When he visited the City and passed among the better class of his color, who in his more popular days had greeted him as "Hon. Rufus Walton" they now alluded to him as "Rufus."

His former constituents argued that while he had posed as their leader and claimed to be pointing the dusky race to a state of more prosperous existence, he had put into practice a theory which was not only condemned by the entire anglo saxon race, but was directly at variance with the principal he was advocating.

Rufus' wife was a woman of German descent, robust, with the glow of health upon her face, and cared little for the condemnation of what she termed "the prejudiced southerners," but Rufus remembering his days in the State in which he first looked upon the world as a free man, and realizing that in his ambition he had pursued a method which would eventually deprive him of his friends, he resolved to return north of the Mason and Dixon line, where he, whose increasing years had increased his knowledge, could be welcomed as a citizen.

CHAPTER XII.

THE "QUEER" MAN.

NOT many years ago on the streets of Washington City one of the most familiar characters seen was an old colored man with long kinky locks which were becoming bleached by Father Time, and while his once stalwart frame was somewhat bent, he bore an air of respectability which marked him as a man of intellect superior to the common ranks of his race. Year followed year, and Rufus with a kindly nature never failed to avail himself of an opportunity to benefit his people, and to brighten the life of some burdened colored being. His declining years were spent quietly, but the old man who found so much that was bright in life, had a smile for every one and an eye for objects of charity.   Alas ! how little genuine charity exists in the world.   If we were to build monuments to all the existing virtues, I fear those representing the other graces in the world would tower above that of charity, like mountains beside a mole hill.

How much more enjoyment some persons find in life than others under similar circumstances, but yet how likely we are to misjudge others regarding their happiness !   While we ofttimes look upon our neighbor and say "If I were only situated as he, how happy would I be," on the other hand, we too often look upon an undemonstrative man who never goes into ecstacies over anything, and who, while he frequently smiles, never laughs out, and we say "poor miserable being, why are some people so droll, and go through life with so little enjoyment." But, not infrequently are those the most contented people.

I once heard a remark made regarding
an intimate friend, which was to the
effect that it was wondered what he lived
for, while as a matter of fact, few men
to whom life seemed brighter could be
found.   He was a man of the type who
are not easy to become acquainted with
and consequently was often misjudged,
while his nature was that possessing an
unusual appreciation of the beautiful,
an ear that heard music in the waterfalls
where others but found terror, and while
he would merely remark upon the beauty
of Nature, his susceptible being received
an impression of the scene in which he
found pleasure in after days.

If the weather in the evening was too
inclement to go out, he would take down
some favorite volume from the library
and spend an evening so pleasantly that
the weather never crossed his mind.
The following day, perhaps by chance
he would meet a friend on the street
who would inquire " well old boy, how

did you spend the miserable rainy evening yesterday?" "Oh! I remained in, read awhile and made the best of it," would be his reply, while the inquiring friend would pass on, thinking "what a strange individual."

We meet two types of men in the common walks of life, either of which we scarcely dare criticise.

The first, the man of the world, "hail fellow well met," makes friends with all whom he meets, is quick to express his opinion and is so open as to readily be understood. He takes the world as it comes, including too often the vices and virtues alike; but the world would miss him — probably because he exists in the majority. The other type, while familiar, is less numerous, who is the "queer" man mentioned, and who is often accused of being selfish to the extent of living in a world of his own, while we simply misunderstand him. He says little (sometimes so little that he may be classed as one of those things which goes without saying) but he sees all that his associates note of the passing events, and in Nature much more.

The last days of Rufus might be compared to the "queer" class, but even on the busy streets where men rush madly to and fro, and can seldom find time to say a kind word to a person in distress, or a small boy with a parcel, inquiring for a certain house, he would always have a spare minute for the benefit of others.

His troubles of the past—his disappointment in politics all ceased to trouble him, but he saw much of the bright and beautiful side of life as he descended its shady incline.

Who cannot look back upon the varying path of life and pointing to a certain period, say, "there was a point where but for a little word spoken by one who little knew their influence, I would have taken the other road," or pointing back say " there was a time when the course of my life was decided by perhaps a single remark from a friend," whether the decision was an advantageous one or otherwise.

Rufus must have appreciated this influence which is wielded more or less by us all, for often when relating a story of adventure to youthful listeners, who were not confined to people of his own color, he endeavored to prevent their forming opinions which were biased or prejudiced.

One evening, to show how blindly we see each other—even our most intimate friends—the old man related a dream as follows ; which had impressed him with the fact that we are prone to view only one side of our associates :

In my vision I entered an old shop, which might appropriately be termed a curiosity shop, standing at the foot of one of the principal Avenues leading to the Capitol.　The shelves and counters were strewn with old books of every description, second-hand paintings the work of artists living generations ago, and all manner of old jewelry and bric-a-brac too numerous to mention.

Although the sun shown brightly outside, the old shop would have been quite dark, except for a short candle which emitted only a hazy flickering light, in which I could see the dust-covered ware. My attention was attracted to a pair of clumsy-looking spectacles lying in a show-case, and as the gray-haired shopkeeper whose frame was bent with age, approached, I inquired about the quaint looking glasses. He straightened up and looked at me with a pair of little squinted eyes for several seconds, which mysterious gaze made me shudder. Finally he deigned to reply, and informed me those were the glasses of good and evil. I hardly grasped his meaning, but he picked up the queer looking spectacles and brushing the dust

of years' accumulation from them,
explained that the lense for the right
eye alone represented the sight of the
charitably inclined portion of the world,
who were few. That lense alone enabled
the human eye to penetrate the inner
man and brought to light every motive
which existed there. It was intensified,
he explained until capable of the most
perfect sight.

The lense for the other eye was that
which exposed the vices of humanity,
which he stated represented the most
natural state of the human eye as
we view each other in our daily lives;
but it was also intensified. With it
could be seen the vilest traits one
possessed. I was seized with a vague
longing to look through the glasses if
only for a moment of time, and especi-
ally did I desire to turn them upon the
mysterious face, therefore I asked to be
permitted to put them on.

"My son, you know not what you

ask " was his reply, " no mortal eye besides my own has ever used those glasses." I plead with the old man to simply allow me to turn them toward the street for a view of only a few seconds.

He looked at me intently for a moment, and said, " young man, to learn you a lesson which you will never forget, you may turn the glasses upon the passing pedestrians, but look straight through the door, and dare not turn them on me, for I am also a man of wickedness."

I placed the spectacles on, and as I beheld a man who paused in front of the shop, I thought I was looking upon an immortal Being, so perfect appeared his deeds. But he passed on.

The other lense being adjusted, I turned the glasses upon another passing mortal, and I will never forget the chill which passed over my body as I beheld every inner motive of what I thought must certainly be the most wicked man on earth. I tore the glasses from my face with a shriek, and waking, realized that I had only been dreaming.

So quiet were the last days of the ex-slave, that when the great reaper of mortality bore him away from our beautiful world to a brighter clime, only a couple of lines in the daily paper mentioned his death as having been a resident of Washington for several years, but none in the city knew much of the eventful life which had just terminated.

Beyond the few who were accustomed to seeing his pleasant face and gray kinky locks upon the street, he was scarcely missed from the city, the scene of a tragedy never to be forgotten, in which he figured.

A Bostonian in Washington one morning read the notice of Rufus' death, to whom the name of the old man was still familiar. He well remembered the circumstances of Rufus' first visit to Boston and the excitement that followed. The Bostonian cummunicated with friends at home, with the result that permission of the widow of the ex-slave was obtained to have his remains interred at Boston, which was done. Only a small slab marks · the final resting place of the first slave to be freed, which bears the name " Rufus Walton."

The obscure mound is generally unnoticed by passers by, but there still remain a few persons who know the history of the negro who was born too ambitious to remain where circumstances placed him ; by whom flowers are occasionally brought to brighten the moss-covered tomb.

THE END.